GO *for* NO!®

YES is the destination.
NO is how you get there!

GO *for* NO!®

Copyright © 2010
by Richard Fenton & Andrea Waltz
All rights reserved.

ISBN 0-9663981-3-0
ISBN 13: 9780966398 137

Published by

C☲URAGECRAFTERS

www.CourageCrafters.com

We Invite You to Visit the Authors at
www.goforno.com
Or Call Us at **866-GOFORNO**

A Small Book with a Big Message

"I first thought, 'How could this little book have anything of value in just 80 pages?' Then, by page 32, I realized that 'this little book' was about to change my life.

"All of my life, I've sought the wisdom that is so precisely laid out in **Go For No!®** *Every other book on the subject of success, handling rejection and building personal character, falls far short of* **Go For No!®**

"Don't read this book unless you are ready to have the greatest success epiphany you've ever experienced. The genius that Richard and Andrea set out is mind blowing. It will change your life, your career and your company.

"If you never read another book as long as you live, then, make **Go For No!®** *your last one. You'll be astounded!"*

- Review by Michael Murphy
www.PositiveAttitudes.com

NO-Quotient™
Personal Assessment

A 20-question profile that takes only a couple minutes to complete, the *Go for No!*® NO-Quotient™ Personal Assessment is an ideal way to test your own perceptions regarding success and failure, complete with a final score to tell you where you landed on our NO-Quotient™ scale. A $20 value… yours **FREE!**

(Enter pin #1050)

Note from the Authors

"GO for NO!" is the fictional story about four unforgettable days in the life of Eric James Bratton... wonderful husband, terrific brother, *and so-so copier salesman.*

It was inspired, to a great degree, by Richard's life experience. As Rich explains: As a kid I had the typical array of dreams; I spent my early years dreaming of becoming a professional baseball player, author and racecar driver just to mention a few. Oh, and yes, like most young boys I loved dinosaurs and would spend hours in the back yard digging for fossils.

One day, at the age of eight, I took my collection of plastic dinosaurs and set them up on a table in my basement and invited everyone in the neighborhood over to hear me talk about them. As I recall, I charged a nickel per person to get in.

As people were leaving one of the parents came up to me and said, *"You are quite the professional speaker!"* I didn't even know what a professional speaker was, but I sure liked the sound of it!

At the age of eight I had discovered my dream.

Over the next thirty years, however, it would remain just that... a dream. I pushed the dream down and pushed it away. I would fantasize about becoming a professional speaker from time to time, dabble in it and flirt with it... everything but actually do it.

Was it the talent? No, I could hold an audience's attention. Was it the desire? No, there was nothing I wanted more. Were there some external forces holding me back? I only wish I could blame it on someone else, but I can't.

What was my problem? My problem was a simple one and all too common... I was afraid of failing. I was afraid of rejection.

In early December of 1997, however, all that changed.

I had just turned forty and was doing some fairly serious review of where life had taken me (where I had *allowed* it to take me, to be more accurate) when I remembered a conversation I had with a supervisor over ten years earlier. It was as if the switch had been flipped and light had suddenly flooded my world and everything became crystal clear.

Several days later I launched my career as a professional speaker and within one year I had written two books, produced five videos and was speaking at conferences for some of the largest companies in America by simply doing what he had told me to do so long ago.

I began to wonder; wouldn't it have been great if the me from ten years earlier, the *me* that had ignored this advice, could have had a conversation with the older, enlightened me? That's when I got the idea for this book.

So, if you could go into the future and talk with yourself... a smarter, bolder, less timid version of you... what would happen? Eric James Bratton is going to get that chance. It will change his life, and if you let it, it can change yours, too.

Richard Fenton & Andrea Waltz

P.S. We also want you to know that, while the main character is a salesman, this book is not only for "salespeople." It's for anyone who has to face rejection; the novelist searching for a publisher, the network marketer building a down line, the entrepreneur looking for venture capital, the student raising money for the softball team or the parent trying to get their kids to eat their peas. *This book is for anyone who wants to break through self-imposed barriers and achieve everything life has to offer.*

"If you're not succeeding fast enough, you're probably not failing fast enough, and you can't have one without the other. So, if you're going to avoid one, you're going to avoid both."

-Joe Malarkey®
The Worst Motivational Speaker in America®
(from **The Go For No!® Movie**)

For Don Fenton Sr.
The Greatest Salesman That Ever Lived

Chapter One...
Starting Off Three for Three

It was the third week of March in 1990.

I turned the steering wheel of the Oldsmobile, guiding it into the parking space next to the empty phone booth. The Cutlass was by no means my preferred choice of vehicles (I'd much rather have opted for a small two-seater), but it was the car my company provided to all its salespeople. There were no exceptions.

This was my third year working for Western Equipment Leasing, and I was doing pretty well for myself. I was twenty-eight, married, and making good money. Not that I was setting the world on fire as a salesman, mind you. I was in the middle of the pack from a performance standpoint, but compared to most of my friends, I had a dream job. As a leasing representative in the copier division, I set my own hours. The sky was the limit in terms of income, and today was a good example of what was possible when I put my mind to it.

I slid a dime in the slot and dialed.

"Good afternoon, Fourth Street Gallery. This is Elaine Bratton."

"Guess what your husband did today!" I grinned widely.

"You picked a bad time to play 20 questions, sweetie. It's really busy, and I have another line on hold."

"Then guess quick."

"Okay, you robbed a bank."

"Close. I made three calls and closed them all. I'm three for three, and it's only Monday! What do you think of that?" I asked.

"Great!" she responded, adding, "maybe we'll be able to put something extra in the Hawaii fund."

"Let's not count our chickens before they're hatched," I said with caution. "I still need one more sale to hit quota. Let me get that notched, and then we'll see."

"Of course. Listen, I really do have to run. Are you picking up dinner or are we cooking?"

"I'm feeling very Chinese, leave it to me."

"I love you. Bye."

"You, too." I hung up the phone and looked at my watch. It was 3:30 in the afternoon, and if memory served me correctly, the Lakers were playing the Knicks at the Garden. I calculated that with the three hour time difference, I could pick up some Kung Pao shrimp and still get home in time for tip off.

Chapter Two...

Tying Up Loose Ends

"Eric! What are you doing here?" the office receptionist called out as I wove my way through the sea of desks on the way to my cubicle Tuesday morning.

"What do you think?" I called back, holding up the mound of papers balanced on my arm. "I'm tying up loose ends, as usual. You know Karen, selling is one-tenth prospecting and nine-tenths paperwork. The more I sell, the more I regret it!"

"Don't let Frank hear you say that," she responded with a smile, motioning to the large office in the corner.

Frank White was Vice President of Sales for WEL and a man not to be taken lightly. A hard-driving, hard-charging type, Frank could instill fear in almost anyone just by looking in their direction. His favorite saying was engraved on a plaque that sat on the edge of his desk for all salespeople to see. It read: *Hit your quota or hit the bricks!* It was intimidation, pure and simple, and for the most part it worked. I couldn't remember the last time I'd missed reaching a sales goal. There were other managers in the company who used carrots to motivate people to perform, but not Frank. Frank was all stick.

The day wore on and eventually the avalanche of paper on my desk began to look like a light snowfall. By about two o'clock in the afternoon, I was caught up on everything and thought I might actually grab a bite to eat and still have time to make a sales call before heading home for the night. I grabbed my jacket and headed down to the basement cafeteria.

After filling my tray with meatloaf, mashed potatoes, a small salad and a Diet Coke, I worked my way to one of the empty tables. No sooner had I put the first bite of food in my mouth, one of the guys from marketing sat down beside me.

"Eric, how's it going, my friend?"

I looked at him suspiciously. No one in sales was ever called "friend" unless there was an ulterior motive. "Fine," I said cautiously. "Tim McDonald, right?"

"Yeah. Tim McDonald. Boy, you guys in sales have great memories! Listen, Eric, I was wondering if you could do me a favor? I'd really owe you."

"What exactly do you need, Tim?"

"We're conducting a focus group of sorts, kind of a cross section of customers and some marketing department people, and we really want to have a representative from sales. Do you think you could spare an hour or so?"

No way, I thought to myself, and almost couldn't believe it when I heard the words, *What time?* roll off my lips.

"Ten a.m. and I promise it won't go over an hour, ninety minutes tops. Thanks." McDonald stood and strode off, getting away quickly before I could change my mind. What a pushover I am. This was really going to put a dent in my day, but an obligation was an obligation I rationalized.

Chapter Three...
That's Why I'm In Sales!

Tim's 10 a.m., *ninety-minute-maximum* focus group finally disbanded at 1:20 in the afternoon and I vowed to never eat in the cafeteria again.

I grabbed some fast food and ate at my desk while looking over a stack of prospect cards, deciding which showed the most promise for the quota-reaching sale I needed to keep the wolves, my wife, and Frank at bay.

The phone rang.

"Hey, it's Carl! Sorry it took so long to get back to you, I was on the road," my brother said.

"Business or pleasure?" I asked, already knowing the answer.

"What's the difference?" he said with a laugh.

"That's your problem, Carl. You don't know how to have fun. And, speaking of fun, that's why I called. I was thinking maybe I should take you up on that invitation to play Bel Air and give you a chance to dust off that membership of yours."

"Sure, the invitation's always open."

"Great! How about you and me playing hooky tomorrow afternoon?"

"No way for tomorrow, not during tax season. Call me in May, and I'm all yours."

"Sorry, Carl, May is no good for me. Right in the middle of copier season, you know," I countered jokingly.

"It's May or no way, little brother," Carl stated resolutely.

"Fine. You pick the Saturday."

"Good. I'll let you know," he said and hung up.

I sat there at my desk, finishing my burger and thinking about how great a round of golf sounded when it suddenly hit me; why not play a round by myself tomorrow? It wouldn't be Bel Air, but golf is golf! If I could get on the course by six, I could be back in the clubhouse by ten and making calls by 11.

I picked up the phone and dialed.

"Strawberry Creek Golf Course," the voice said.

"Yeah, I was hoping to get an early tee time tomorrow morning," I began.

"Got nothing before ten-thirty," the voice replied.

I was just about to say 'no thanks' to the voice when I remembered that I only needed one more sale to bring in the week. If I were to tee off at ten-thirty, I'd still be able to make two calls between three o'clock and five o'clock.

"Ten-thirty," I responded.

* * *

After dinner that night, I went to the garage to load my clubs in the trunk when Elaine came through, garbage bags in each hand.

"You playing this weekend?" she asked.

"Nope. Tomorrow morning," I beamed.

"Tomorrow? Boy, I wish I could take off in the middle of the week to play golf," she said playfully, pushing the lid down on the overflowing trashcan.

"That's why I'm in sales, Laney. That's why I'm in sales!"

"Well, Mr. Palmer, I don't mind you playing golf, but you'd better..."

"Don't worry," I said, cutting her off. "I've still got two and a half days to hit quota. I never miss, do I?"

"No, you never miss. You're a great salesman Eric, but a lousy psychic. I was going to say that you'd better not forget to take the cans to the curb before you leave. Tomorrow's trash day!"

Later that evening, lying in bed, I said to my wife, "I've decided not to take the garbage out tomorrow."

"And why is that?" she asked incredulously.

"Because," I said with great fanfare, "garbage day isn't until Thursday!"

"Eric, my love, tomorrow is Thursday."

"No it's not! It's Wednesday!"

"Sorry. You've lost a day," she replied, returning to her Reader's Digest.

Thursday? How could tomorrow be Thursday already? But she was right of course. Monday was the day I'd made three sales, Tuesday I spent doing paperwork in the office, and today I got tied up in that stupid focus group. Tomorrow was indeed Thursday. My week was evaporating around me, and to add insult to injury, I was planning to play golf in the morning. Well, I thought, I'll just have to play quick, that's all there is to it.

With that, I closed my eyes and drifted off to a peaceful sleep with visions of birdies and eagles dancing in my head...

Chapter "Fore"...

Strawberry Creek

... I found myself standing at the 14th tee, a 172-yard par 3. I had played this hole twenty times and never birdied it, not even once, but today was going to be different.

Having been all over the place with my irons, I decided I'd use my three wood. I'd just take a gentle, easy swing and plop this shot right on the middle of the green.

The ball sailed high in the air and then started its downward trajectory toward the green. I could see already that the shot was going to be long, the three wood had been too much club. If the ball did hit the green at all, it was going to be at the very back edge. "Stick! Stick!" I shouted, attempting to will the little round sphere to stop in its tracks as it hit, but it had other thoughts in mind. The green was very hard, the morning dew having burned off many hours earlier, and the ball skipped off and sailed down the steep slope that led directly towards Strawberry Creek (for which the course was named). Suddenly my birdie two was looking like a bogey four, and that was assuming I wasn't in the water.

I stepped onto the stones that littered the bank of the creek and peered in. Yep, that was my Titleist all right. There would be no salvaging this hole I thought as I turned to retrieve the ball scoop from my bag. Suddenly I felt the cleats of my shoes slip on the mossy rocks, and all at once I lost my balance, both feet going out from under me at the same time.

I remembered thinking as I went backwards into the icy water how I hoped nobody was watching this display of clumsiness. Then, as I felt my head connect with a gigantic rock on the creek-bottom, with everything going black around me, how much I hoped that someone was watching after all.

Chapter Five

What On Earth is Happening

As I slowly came to my senses, I couldn't decide which hurt more: my hip, which took the brunt of the impact as I hit the hardwood floor, or the back of my head, which must have caught the edge of the nightstand.

"Jeez! I really whacked myself a good one," I said to Elaine, holding the back of my throbbing head. "I don't think I've fallen out of bed since grade school!"

I padded slowly toward the bedroom door, exaggerating my hip injury for sympathy, but Elaine remained mute.

"I'm going to go get some ice for this," I said even more loudly, but still there was no response. Then, peering through the darkness, the realization hit me... Elaine wasn't in bed. As I flipped the light switch on the wall, a cold wave of fear came over me. Not only was the bed empty, but it wasn't my bed. It wasn't even our room!

Confusion and fear grew with every step as I made my way out into the hallway. Exotic art hung from the walls and the carpet felt strangely thick under my feet. At the end of the hallway I noticed two large sliding glass doors. I flipped the latch and walked out onto a large terrace overlooking a beautiful golf course.

Feeling somewhat dizzy, I made my way over to a pair of padded chaise lounges and lowered myself into one of them. What is happening to me? I wondered. What on Earth is happening here? Then, feeling very tired; I closed my eyes and drifted off to sleep as the sun rose silently over the perfectly manicured green below.

Chapter Six…

You Don't Look So Good

It was mid-morning when I awoke, the sun shining brightly on my face and my stomach growling from hunger.

I slid the glass door open and heard someone singing downstairs. "Elaine? Is that you?" I called out, but there was no response.

Following the singing, I made my way down a large spiral staircase, across a marbled foyer and into a mammoth kitchen to discover a woman who clearly was not my wife. She was older, probably in her fifties, heavy set, and dressed in a white maid's uniform.

"Excuse me," I said, catching her off guard. She spun around quickly, losing her grip on the large ceramic platter she was drying, sending it crashing to the floor.

"Mr. Bratton! I'm sorry, but you startled me. I didn't expect you to be here so late in the morning," she said.

"I'm sorry," I said apologetically, "I thought you were my wife."

"Mrs. Bratton is in Europe," she responded, collecting colorful chunks of ceramic from the floor.

"Europe?" I inquired, bending over to help her pick up the shattered dish. "What is Elaine doing in Europe?"

"I believe she's buying art," the maid responded suspiciously, "at least that's what I was told."

"By whom? Who told you that?" I queried.

"Well, by you! Mr. Bratton, are you okay?"

"I'm fine, why?"

"Because you don't look so good."

"I hit my head on the nightstand; it's nothing."

"I think you should have it looked at. Would you like me to call the doctor?"

"No, I'm fine," I said, waving her off. "I'll just rest a bit."

I went into the bathroom to wash my face. Looking up, I caught my reflection in the mirror. "Oh my God!" I gasped. The maid was right. I didn't look so good. The person in the mirror was me, but then again it wasn't. It was an older version of me. My hair contained touches of gray and creases were evident in my face where none were before.

I made my way back to the master bedroom where I had awoken and stepped in front of the three-way mirror. I could see that I was carrying at least twenty extra pounds on my five-foot nine-inch frame, and whatever muscle tone I once had was clearly gone.

I hurried back downstairs in a panic and found the maid busy vacuuming the living room rug.

"Excuse me!" I shouted.

"Yes, sir?" she said, flipping the off switch to the vacuum.

"What's your name?"

She gave me a puzzled look before responding, "Why, it's Renee, sir. Are you sure you're okay?"

"No, Renee, I am not okay. I am not okay at all! Listen, I need to ask you a few questions, and as strange or as ridiculous as they may seem, I need you to answer them, okay?"

"Okay," she said hesitantly.

"Good. My name is Eric Bratton, correct?"

"Yes, sir."

"This is my house, and you work for me?"

"Yes, sir," she said, a combination of concern and fear beginning to show in her eyes.

"And what do I do for a living?"

"Well, as I understand it, you're a business man." Then she added, "Oh, yes, and you write books."

"What did you just say?"

"You write books."

"That's not true," I blurted. I mean, I barely have time to read books let alone write one. "I don't write books. I sell copiers for a living!"

"With all due respect, Mr. Bratton, I clean the house three days a week, including the study, and I've seen the books you've written."

I ran up the spiral staircase to the second floor and tried several doors before locating the study. Making my way to the bookshelves, I began searching, and there they were… three hardcover books, sitting side by side. *Fail Your Way to Success; One of These Days Is Now!; How to Have the Most Productive Year of Your Life.* And, there on the spine, was my name… Eric James Bratton.

My mind raced. Certainly there's more than one Eric Bratton in the world, but how many Eric James Brattons could there be?

Reaching up, I plucked one of the titles from the shelf and leafed through it quickly, not recognizing any of the words as my own. Then, as I flipped it over, I stopped dead in my tracks. On the back cover of the dust jacket was a picture of the author.

It was a photo of me.

Chapter Seven...
The Other Me

Weak kneed, I sat down in a large leather chair, turned to the author biography page, and studied the words:

Eric James Bratton is a one-time clothing salesman whose meteoric rise to the top of the corporate ladder is the American Dream! As a leasing representative for Western Equipment Leasing, Eric Bratton shattered every sales record imaginable. His first book, Fail Your Way to Success (published in 1989 by Simon & Schuster) was an overnight success and quickly became the bible for salespeople everywhere. In 1994, he accepted the number three spot at duplication behemoth CopyQuest to become the youngest Vice President in the organization's thirty-year history. An avid golfer and marathon runner, he lives with his wife Elaine (a prominent West Coast art dealer) in La Costa, California. This is his third book.

His first book published in 1989! How could that be? I walked over to the desk and looked at the calendar: March 23, 2000. I touched my face, realizing that somehow it was now ten years later, and I was ten years older. No wonder I looked so bad!

Then at the bottom of the page I noticed this:

For more information, he can be reached at 800-290-5028.

Without hesitation I went to the desk, picked up the telephone and dialed. The phone rang only once.

"Good afternoon, CopyQuest!"

"Uh, yes. May I speak with Eric Bratton?"

"Certainly. May I say who's calling?"

"Sure. Tell him it's… a close friend. *A very close friend.*"

"One moment please."

I was placed on hold, but in seconds she was back.

"Mr. Bratton is just finishing up a call. I'll put you through shortly."

"Thank you," I said, my heart racing. What am I going to say? I wondered. He'll probably just hang up. I know I would.

I was just about ready to hang up the phone myself when his voice, self-assured and pleasant, came on the line.

"Good afternoon, Eric Bratton."

"Yes, Mr. Bratton. I was hoping you could help me with something."

"Certainly, but who is this?"

"Sure, but first promise me you won't hang up, at least until you've heard everything I have to say."

"Your voice sounds familiar, but I can't place from where."

"Well, it should. My name is Eric Bratton. Eric James Bratton, born December 2, 1962 in Anchorage, Alaska."

"I don't know what this game is but I'm not going to play. Please don't call here again," he said curtly.

"Wait!" I shouted into the receiver. "I don't understand this any more than you do, but I went to bed last night in my apartment and woke up this morning in your house."

"That's impossible."

"Impossible, huh? Do you have a private line in your study?"

"That's none of your business," he snapped.

"I'll take that as a yes. I want you to call it right now."

"And why should I do that?"

"Because I'm sitting at your desk, and that seems the best way to prove it to you," I said and hung up.

Ten seconds passed. I was just about convinced he wasn't going to call when the phone rang. I grabbed the receiver.

"I know you're probably tempted to call the police," I began, "but I want to tell you something which only you would know. In the seventh grade, you borrowed an album from your best friend, Steve. The next day he asked if you took it but you lied, and to avoid getting caught you broke it into small pieces and buried it in your back yard. But the next morning you felt so guilty, you bought a replacement that you left on his front porch. And you never told a soul."

"Out of curiosity," he asked quietly, "who was the group?"

"Tommy James and the Shondells."

"I'll be there in fifteen minutes."

Chapter Eight...
Looking in the Mirror

When he walked in the door to the study, it was like looking into a mirror. Except for the fact that he was immaculately dressed, tanned and about twenty pounds lighter, he and I were identical twins.

After studying me for several seconds, he placed his briefcase on the desk and loosened his necktie.

"You weren't kidding, were you?" he said finally.

"I wish I were," I responded gravely.

"I don't usually drink in the afternoon, but I think I'm going to make an exception. You want one?" he asked, making his way over to the small bar on the other side of the study.

"Sure."

"Why don't you start from the top and tell me everything," he said as he handed me a Scotch rocks and slid into the leather chair opposite me.

"Starting where?" I asked, "from early childhood, or this morning? Which, by the way, was ten years ago for me!"

"Wherever you want to start is fine."

*   *   *

It took a full hour to cover everything, and during that time he didn't say a word – he just nodded every so often to let me know he was listening.

"So what do you think?" I asked.

"I think it's amazing! Don't you?"

"Yeah, well I guess. I'd probably be a little more amused if it were the other way around, if *you* woke up on *my* bedroom floor."

"Well, *Eric*, I don't believe that anything happens by accident. And while I won't begin to pretend to know why this is happening,

I'm sure there *is* a reason. Sooner or later, we'll figure it out!" he said with a sense of certainty.

Though I'm not sure that I really believed him, I did like the confident tone of his voice and felt more at ease for his having said it.

He looked at his watch. "I have an important meeting at four-thirty," he said, "which should be over no later than six p.m. I'll meet you back here and we'll go to dinner and try to figure this thing out. In the meantime you sit tight, relax, and make yourself at home!"

I laughed at the thought of making myself at home in a house that was owned by an *alternative-reality-me* and I felt some tension release.

"And take whatever clothing you need," he offered.

"The pants might be a bit tight," I said, placing my hand on my waist, "but I'm sure I can find something that will work."

"Good. I'll see you about six-thirty, and save your appetite. We'll go somewhere nice, downtown maybe."

"Don't worry, I'm famished."

I was beginning to like the other me already.

Chapter Nine...
Oh Yeah, Elaine!

No sooner had the other Eric Bratton pulled out of the drive in his shiny black Jaguar that the phone began to ring. My first instinct was to reach over and answer it; after all, I was Eric Bratton, too! But I restrained myself. After the third ring the answer machine clicked on.

It was a woman's voice, a voice I knew instantly and intimately. It was my wife.

"Hey, it's me! I'm calling here because the office said you went home for some reason," she began. *"I hope everything's okay. Listen, I only have a minute* (some things haven't changed, I thought), *but I wanted to let you know that things are going great. I made an unbelievable purchase of thirty pieces in Florence, and tomorrow I'm off to Madrid. Call me at the hotel later; don't worry about the time. Love you. Bye."*

The answer machine clicked off. I'd been so wrapped up in my dilemma, I completely forgot about Elaine. *My* Elaine, I mean. His Elaine was apparently doing just fine, living her dream of traveling the world and buying art, but what was *my* Elaine doing? I wondered. Was she worried? Did she even exist anymore? Only time would tell.

I spent the rest of the afternoon reading one of *my* books, trying to make sense of the situation. It was amazing.

Chapter Ten...
Dinner at Rainwater's

"I can't believe how the skyline has changed in only ten years," I commented as we exited the freeway toward downtown San Diego.

"And the traffic!" he chimed in.

We pulled up to valet parking at *Rainwater's on Kettner*, a well-known restaurant near the gaslamp district which I had always wanted to visit but never had the opportunity or the means. After we were seated, Eric chose a nice bottle of Stag's Leap Cabernet which we sipped while waiting for our steaks to arrive.

"I read our book today," I started with a laugh.

"Oh yeah, which one?"

"*Fail Your Way to Success*," I responded.

"And what did you think?"

"Honestly? I liked it."

He smiled and looked truly pleased as the waiter placed our steaks in front of us.

"Did you discover any clues, anything that might explain why this is happening?"

"Perhaps. From what I can tell, virtually everything in our lives has been identical. We were both born on the same day to the same parents, and we have an older brother named Carl. We grew up in the same neighborhood, went to the same schools and had the same teachers. We worked the same jobs during high school, and we both sold suits at Dubin's Clothing for Men during college. But then something happened…"

"What do you mean, *something* happened?" he asked.

"All the experiences you wrote about in your book were identical to mine, that is, right up until the job at the clothing store," I responded. "It's at that point that things changed somehow."

"What changed?"

"Well, in the book you mentioned an encounter you had with the district manager, a guy named Harold. Do you remember?"

"Do I remember? How could I forget? That's the day that changed my life!" he exclaimed.

"That's the problem. That day never happened to me."

"What do you mean? How can a day *not* happen?"

"Of course that day *happened*, it just didn't happen the same way for me as it did for you."

"You mean to say you don't remember the conversation with Harold that day?" he asked incredulously.

"Honestly, I couldn't begin to tell you a single thing Harold said," I replied.

"Wow! Then maybe that's where we need to start!"

Chapter Eleven...

Then How Did You Know He Was Done?

"I remember it like it was yesterday," the other Eric began. "I, or *we*, had only been working at Dubin's for about a month when the district manager, Harold, was scheduled to do a store visit and I really wanted to impress him. As you may remember, we weren't doing very well sales-wise," he recounted, "and quite honestly I was worried that if my personal sales didn't improve that they were going to let me go. This is right after Elaine and I got married, and the last thing I needed was to suddenly be without a job."

"I remember it well," I said in agreement.

"Harold showed up about nine-thirty in the morning and everybody said their hellos, coffee and donuts and all that, and at ten o'clock we opened the doors. I was the first salesman in that morning so I had first ups. Sound familiar so far?"

I nodded.

"Then," he continued, "in walks this finely-dressed gentleman who announces that he wants to buy an entire wardrobe of clothing! And, within thirty minutes, I have my biggest sale ever. I was certain that Harold would be impressed."

"I remember that too," I said.

"After the customer left, Harold finally sauntered over and said, '*Nice sale kid.*' My chest puffed out with pride. 'Eleven hundred dollars!' I proclaimed. But Harold just stood there and didn't seem overly impressed. Finally he said, '*I'm just curious, but what did that customer say no to?*' 'What do you mean?' I shot back. 'That guy just bought a suit, sport coat, three shirts, six ties, shoes, socks, a belt and underwear! What do you mean, what did he say *no* to?'

"Harold waited calmly for me to stop being defensive, then he said, '*We've already established what he said yes to. What I want to know now is, what did he say no to?*'

"I thought for a long time, mentally reviewing the sale in my mind, then sheepishly I replied, 'Nothing. That customer didn't say *no* to anything.' '*So,*' Harold asked, '*then how did you know he was done?*'

"His question hit me like a punch because I suddenly realized the customer hadn't ended the sale, I had! Why? For only one reason I could think of… the customer had hit my mental spending limit. I realized that I had never spent more than a thousand bucks on a shopping trip ever, so when anyone went over my mental spending limit, *hey… they were done!*"

"I pretty much remember that," I said, "but it didn't have that much impact on me. That's what changed your life?"

"Yes. That and what Harold said next. He said, '*The salesperson never decides when the sale is over; the customer does.*' Then he looked me in the eye and said, '*Eric, your fear of hearing the word 'no' is the only thing standing between you and greatness.*'

"It was amazing. I had gone into work that morning hoping to keep my job, and I went home that night just two letters away from greatness."

Two letters from greatness, I heard myself repeating.

N and O.

No.

Chapter Twelve...
The Failure / Success Model

"You see, before that moment with Harold," my alter ego continued, "I had been operating with the wrong model of success and failure. I thought that..."

He stopped mid-sentence and signaled the waiter to clear the plates and at the same time borrowed his pen.

"I thought that I was here, in the middle, with success on one end and failure on the other," he said drawing on the back of the restaurant menu:

SUCCESS ← ← ← ME → → → FAILURE

"I had always thought my mission was to do everything within my power to move toward success... and to move away from failure. But that moment with Harold opened my eyes. I realized that the correct model looked like this," he said, attacking the menu once again with the pen:

ME → → → FAILURE → → → SUCCESS

"I realized that failure was the halfway mark on the road to success, not a destination to be avoided but rather a stepping stone to get what I really wanted in life. Most people get to the sign marked 'failure' and they figure they're heading in the wrong direction, turn around and head back home. They think that success must be back the other way, but it's not! It's straight ahead!

"I read somewhere that great leaders never use the word failure. Instead, they use words like mistake, glitch or setback. This is silly and counterproductive. The word *fail* may have four letters in it, but it's not a *four-letter word!* When people use cute substitutes, they treat it as if it were. '*We tried but we hit a glitch!*' they say. Give me a break! Just say you failed! Big deal! Is that so hard? No wonder everyone on the planet thinks failing is something to be avoided at all costs. We sugarcoat it and dance around it and talk about it as if it were death! The best way to desensitize yourself to a word is to use it, and the best way to desensitize yourself to an action is to do it!"

I sat there watching this man extolling the virtues of failing as if he were a zealot on a crusade, a man who until just minutes ago I thought was very much like me. But we were very different indeed.

"It's the same thing with the word *no*," he continued. "As kids we weren't phased at all when we heard the word *no*, were we? Every Saturday morning in grocery stores all across America you can hear kids passing right through failure and taking *no* in stride on their way to success...

Billy:	*Can I have a cookie, mommy?*
Mom:	*No.*
Billy:	*I want a cookie!*
Mom:	*No.*
Billy:	*Please can I have a cookie?*
Mom:	*No.*
Billy:	*Please?*
Mom:	*I said no!*
Billy:	*Pretty please with sugar on top?*
Mom:	*No, no, no!*
Billy:	*Why can't I have a cookie?*
Mom:	*Because I said so.*
Billy:	*But why?*
Mom:	*Listen to me, young man. I am not going to say this again. The answer is N-O!*

Ten seconds later...

Billy:	*Mommy, I want a cookie!*
Mom:	*Oh, for heaven's sake, just one!*

"Have you ever witnessed this?" he asked.

"All the time," I said laughing hysterically.

"Sure you do, we all do! The thing is, not only does Billy get his cookie, but what has he learned in the process?"

"That if he pushes long enough and hard enough and doesn't quit, there's a *yes* at the end of the cookie trail," I replied.

"Exactly! Now I'm not saying that adults should act like spoiled brats to get what they want, but there is an important lesson to be learned here. Somewhere along the line that natural sense of tenacity we had as children got drummed out of us. Billy knows not to take the rejection personally, but as adults we forget that. That's what Harold helped me remember.

Chapter Thirteen...

Where Our Paths Parted

"After the conversation with Harold I started really looking at what set successful people apart from the masses, and their willingness to fail was at the top of the list. Statistically, only five percent of the population will be able to retire without assistance," he stated. "Thirty-six percent will have already died, six will continue working, and a staggering fifty-three percent will be dependent on friends, relatives, government or charity for their survival. And who do you think gets to be in the lucky five percent? The people who failed the most during their lifetimes, that's who!"

"It's pretty ironic." I said.

"Yes. Ironic, and sad. Repeat after me, Eric... I like to fail."

"That's my problem. I don't like to fail."

"That's because you still think that failing leads to failure. Failing... *and becoming a failure...* are two very different things. Successful people fail eagerly while failures avoid failing. The whole point of becoming willing to fail more is to become a success, so that one day you won't be forced to look back on your life and say to yourself, *'I'm a failure.'* Do you understand that?"

"Yes," I said.

"Good. Then repeat after me: I like to fail."

"I like to fail," I said half-heartedly.

"I fail big and I fail often."

"I fail big and I fail often," I repeated.

"Sticks and stones may break my bones, but '*no*' can never hurt me!"

I couldn't control myself and burst out laughing.

"Say it, or I'll make you pick up the check!"

"Okay, okay. Sticks and stones may break my bones, but '*no*' can never hurt me."

"Good. The word *no* doesn't have to be debilitating to us. That's the most important lesson you'll ever learn, Eric. Harold tried to teach you that, but you weren't ready yet. Are you ready now?"

I nodded.

"If that's true, then from this second forward your life will never be the same."

I sat there for a moment, pondering if I really believed him, if I really believed that making such a subtle change in attitude could truly change my life. Then I thought of something that I needed to know desperately, though I was pretty sure I could guess.

"What happened after the conversation with Harold?" I asked.

"Well, as I recall, that night I went home and told Elaine that we'd never have to worry about money again for as long as we lived!"

"No. I mean, what happened with the job?" I asked weakly.

"I went into work the next morning a new man. I was on fire! I finished the year as the number one salesman in the store and the following year as the number one in the chain. You don't remember that?"

"No, I don't remember that. Because that's not what happened next for me."

"What happened to you?" he asked.

"My sales didn't improve. As a matter of fact, they got worse. Two months later I was fired."

*   *   *

We sat in silence, each of us pondering the significance of an event that had changed one life so positively and had apparently not altered the direction of the other in the slightest.

Finally, the waiter brought the check and I watched as Eric James Bratton, the man who became a success by embracing failure, signed the credit card receipt and placed his platinum American Express card back in his billfold. As we were leaving, I noticed the waiter eyeing the scribbled menu. I'm sure he was wondering to himself, 'What in the heck is this?'

It's the difference between massive success and mediocre performance! I wanted to tell him. *It's your future, one way or the other!* I wanted to shout.

And I knew, in that instant, that for me it would always be the lesson I was privileged enough to be offered a decade ago but chose to ignore. I had proved the old saying true: Some people stumble over the truth, pick themselves up, and go on their merry way as if nothing had happened at all.

Chapter Fourteen...

An Invitation I Couldn't Refuse

I spent Thursday night in the guest bedroom. Early the next morning I heard a knock and Eric's voice informing me that breakfast was served.

We talked about the weather and sports over fresh fruit and muffins, but soon the conversation made its way back to what we had begun to refer to as "*the situation.*"

"I spoke to Elaine this morning," he began.

"Did you tell her about *the situation*?" I asked.

"No, I didn't. I couldn't see the point in worrying her."

"Because she'd think you were crazy?"

"Something like that. Speaking of situations, we need to make some arrangements."

"Are you kicking me out?"

"No, of course not. *Mi casa es su casa*, at least until Elaine returns from Spain which won't be until Tuesday night. If you're still here at that time it could get complicated, but for now we just need to plan the next several days."

"Whatever you say is fine with me," I offered.

"Good. I've got a pretty full schedule today. I've got an eight o'clock flight to Monterey for a presentation I have to give tomorrow in San Francisco. You can hang out here and relax, but you're invited to come along. The decision is yours."

"Well, if it's all the same to you, I'd like to come along." I'd feel awkward alone in the house, the maid trying to vacuum under my feet and wondering why I still looked ill. "It will give me a chance to pick your brain some more."

"Then it's settled."

"Just remember that I've got no money," I interjected, somewhat embarrassed. "I don't usually put my wallet in my PJ's on the off chance I might accidentally fall out of bed and land in another part of the space-time continuum."

"No problem," he said with a laugh. Then he asked, "By the way, do you still play golf?"

"Absolutely!"

"Good. How would you like to play eighteen holes with two of my top salespeople and me tomorrow? We've got a seven-thirty tee-time at Pebble Beach. You'd make it a foursome."

"Are you kidding? Pebble Beach!" I gasped.

"I'll take that as a yes."

"But what are you going to tell them, about me I mean?"

"Let's tell them the truth. We'll just say you're my twin."

Chapter Fifteen...
A Time for Reflection

I spent the good part of that morning perusing my way through books that wouldn't be published for many years (at least to me, they wouldn't) and watching people with lives more desperate than mine on daytime talk shows that had clearly gone downhill over the years. But mostly I found myself reflecting on the previous evening's conversation and mourning over the years I wasted operating with a false, ineffective model of success and failure. The way I had squandered my time seemed almost criminal.

I made my way back to the study and pulled the copy of *Fail Your Way to Success* from the bookshelf, deciding to review the concepts again in a little more detail. And this time I read the book from cover to cover, word for word. After all, who knew if one day I would suddenly wake up in my own bed and kick myself for not having studied harder!

In the back of the book I found a fold out chart with the heading, *The Five Failure Levels*, and suddenly had a great inspiration. I ripped the sheet from the book and folded it in half several times, placing it in the front pocket of my trousers. In movies the time-traveler always brings back proof that he's been to another dimension. If I were ever able to return home to *my* Elaine and *my* life in 1990, this page would be my proof!

I closed the book and looked at the clock. It was getting late and the car would be coming shortly to take me to the airport for the flight to Monterey.

The FIVE FAILURE Levels...

Level 1... The Ability to Fail

100% of the people on the planet Earth have the ability to fail... it's where we all start!

What keeps most people at Level One status is their intense desire to *avoid* any form of failure at all costs. As a result, 80% of all people never move past this basic level.

Level 2... Willingness to Fail

Level Two people develop the willingness to fail, which means that they come to *accept* failure as a natural by product of the process of seeking success.

Fewer than 20% of all people make it to Level Two for any sustained period of time.

Level 3... Wantingness to Fail

Having the *wantingness* to fail goes beyond mere tolerance or acceptance of failure as a part of life... *wantingness* means developing the *desire to fail* with the inner faith that personal and financial growth will follow.

Fewer than 5% of all people ever get to Level Three.

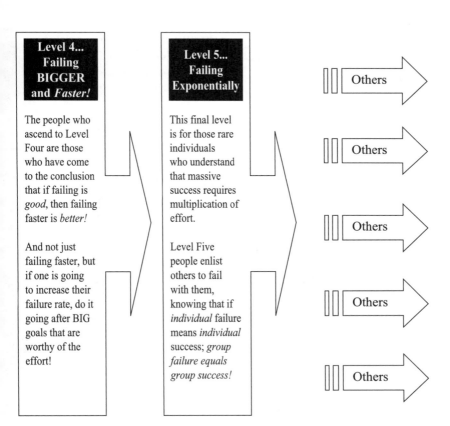

**Level 4...
Failing
BIGGER
and *Faster!***

The people who ascend to Level Four are those who have come to the conclusion that if failing is *good*, then failing faster is *better!*

And not just failing faster, but if one is going to increase their failure rate, do it going after BIG goals that are worthy of the effort!

**Level 5...
Failing
Exponentially**

This final level is for those rare individuals who understand that massive success requires multiplication of effort.

Level Five people enlist others to fail with them, knowing that if *individual* failure means *individual* success; *group failure equals group success!*

Others

Others

Others

Others

Others

...and What it Takes to Progress Through Them!

Chapter Sixteen…

This Is Your Captain Speaking

The limousine was right on time and I was whisked off to the airport. What I didn't expect was to be let out next to a small four-passenger jet at the edge of a private airstrip in the middle of nowhere.

"What's wrong with you?" Eric asked.

"Well, for starters, I have a personal policy to never fly in anything that would fit it my garage," I joked, trying to disguise my fear as I eyed the small plane.

"Oh, yeah! I was afraid of small planes at one time, wasn't I?" he said mostly to himself. "Well, it's too late to do anything about it now, so hop in!"

"Uh, where's the pilot?" I asked.

"Captain Bratton, at your service," he said with a bow.

"You mean to say I fly *planes* in the future?" I asked in utter disbelief.

"Not if you keep letting your fears get in the way, you don't! Now get in."

I climbed hesitantly into the plane and belted myself in as my daredevil twin started the engine. Soon we were rolling down the runway and heading toward heaven.

"There's a song out now with a line in it that says, '*Do something everyday that scares you,*'" he called over the hum of the engine as the plane continued its climb. "Isn't that great?"

"Swell. I've had my scare for the day, so can we land now?" I asked through clenched teeth.

"Quit focusing on your fear and look at the positive, Eric."

"Which is?"

"You're expanding your comfort zone. You know the comfort zone is never static. It's always in a state of expansion or retraction. Think about how courageous you're being."

"I'm not being courageous, I'm shaking in fear!"

"Courage is not the absence of fear," he stated. "Courage is acting in the face of fear. It's being afraid of something and doing it anyway."

"*Do the thing and ye shall have the power!*" I said in the voice of a mock evangelist.

"Amen," my twin replied.

For the next ten minutes I kept *acting* as brave as I could. And eventually, just as he predicted, my fear began to subside and in time, I actually began to enjoy the flight.

"You look like you're relaxing a bit."

"Yeah, my heart rate is finally under a hundred," I quipped.

"Good. It will take me a couple of minutes to get us to altitude and get the autopilot engaged. Then we'll talk."

I continued watching out the tiny window as he pushed buttons, turned knobs and communicated with the tower as we glided over the Pacific Ocean, banking to the right and heading northward up the coast toward Monterey.

Chapter Seventeen…

Learning to "Go for No!"

"So you're really trying to tell me that your willingness to hear the word *no* made everything you're enjoying in your life right now possible?" I asked.

"No, Eric, I'm not saying that at all. My willingness to hear *no* got me on the right track in my career, but it was my *wantingness to fail* that catapulted me to the top," he responded.

"I read this in the book, but explain the difference to me again."

"Sure. A willingness to fail means a person will tolerate just enough failure to get what they *need* from life, and no more. A *wantingness*, on the other hand, means you're not just tolerating the *no's* in your life, you're actually beginning to seek them. When you develop a true wantingness to fail, rejection starts being fun!"

"Who in their right mind thinks rejection is fun? Rejection is awful!" I argued.

"Says who?" he shot back. "Where is it written that rejection has to be *awful*? Why can't rejection be only slightly *annoying* or *amusing* or, for that matter, *exciting* and *energizing*? While we have absolutely no control over the actions of others, we do have total and complete control over how we react. What if we decided to make each *no* we received and every rejection we encountered something that *empowers* us? Instead of avoiding rejection, what if we made the decision to seek rejection? Instead of avoiding *no* or perhaps simply tolerating it, what if we went out of our way to actually *go for no!*"

Chapter Eighteen...

The Most Empowering Word in the World

"Wait a minute. Did you say, *go for no*?" I asked.

"Yes," he responded matter-of-factly.

"How does that work?"

"Simple. Rather than setting goals for the number of *yes's* you are planning to get each week, you set goals for the number of *no's* you're going to collect."

"Now that's crazy!"

"You want crazy? One of the salespeople we're going to play golf with tomorrow morning has a license plate that reads N♥WTHNO: *In love with no*. You know why? Last year he won the award for getting rejected by more prospects than any other salesperson in the company."

"You give an award for failing?" I asked.

"Sure. It's one of our organization's top honors. At the annual awards banquet not only did he get a trophy, but he also received a standing ovation from his peers."

"Praise from your peers for failing. Now I've heard everything!"

"No you haven't. When he got back to his table he placed the award for the greatest number of *no's* right next to the award for being the top salesperson in the country."

"You mean to tell me the guy on your sales force who failed the most was also the number one salesman in the company?" I asked in disbelief.

"Four years in a row," he said.

"That's amazing!"

"Yes, and it's what I've been trying to tell you. A few years ago we hired a well-known motivational speaker for our annual sales conference. In the middle of the presentation the speaker proceeds to tell the group that the most empowering word in the English language is the word yes. Then he had everybody stand and chant, *Yes! Yes! Yes! Yes! Yes!* at the top of their lungs, and I have to admit it was very charging. I mean, the energy was flowing and it was all very motivating indeed. The problem, of course, was that he was absolutely, positively wrong!"

"What did you do?"

"I couldn't allow eight hundred salespeople to walk out with their heads screwed on backwards, so I did the only thing I could think of. When the speaker was done and gone I climbed on the stage and told everyone he was wrong, that the most empowering word in the world is *not* yes... the most empowering word in the world is *NO!*

"I told them that hearing yes is the easy part of the job and teaches you virtually nothing. But learning to hear *no* over and over again and to never quit... now *that* builds character and self-esteem. *That's empowering!*"

"Two letters from greatness," I said, remembering our conversation from the previous night.

"That's right. And the letters are..."

"N-O!"

Chapter Nineteen...

Setting "NO" Goals

"Would you agree that the average salesperson slows down when he or she reaches their quota?" my mentor asked.

"Yes," I replied.

"Why do you think that is?"

"They're rewarding themselves for their accomplishment, I guess."

"Rewarding themselves by ruining their chances at having a record breaking week or month? No, I think it's just another way of staying within comfort zones and avoiding the pain of rejection. Most people classify the amount of pain they must endure to survive in this world as *necessary* pain. Anything beyond that, by definition, is unnecessary pain. That's why it becomes so easy to dodge that extra effort, we've labeled it in our minds as *unnecessary*."

"That's exactly what I did this week," I finally admitted. "I had a great Monday going. I was three for three, and what did I do? I spent Tuesday doing paperwork, Wednesday in a focus group, and on Thursday I was going to play golf, until I fell out of bed and wound up here, that is."

"Ben Franklin said it best: *Success has ruined many a man*."

"Yeah, well I let having a great day turn into a horrible week."

"Let's look at what would have happened if you were setting *no goals* rather than yes goals."

"Okay."

"What was your sales goal for the week?"

"My goal was to close four sales," I replied.

"And how many calls do you usually make in a typical week?"

"I try to get myself in front of twenty prospects every week."

"Okay. So what if, instead of having the goal of getting four yes's, your goal had been to get a minimum of sixteen *no's*. What would have happened on Monday afternoon after you closed your third sale?"

"Instead of being ahead I'd have been behind!" I exclaimed.

"Correct. So what would you have had to do?"

"I'd have had to *increase* the number of calls if I was ever going to get to sixteen *no's* for the week!"

"Exactly! Your success would have led to an increased number of calls, whereas when you were going for *yes* you decreased them."

"I get it!" I said excitedly. "Let's use my friend Paul who is in network marketing, for example. If his goal is to get ten people per week to come to a meeting, and typically about five percent of the people he approaches are willing to attend, then his goal would be to get one hundred and ninety people to say 'no thanks.'"

"Yes. His goal would be to get rejected by one hundred and ninety people. You might call it the *get rejected and get rich plan.*"

"Get rejected and get rich," I repeated quietly to myself.

"Eric, I'm going to tell you the truth. I haven't set a traditional success-oriented goal in almost ten years. I only set goals for the number of *no's* I'm going to get."

"You set no success goals at all?" I asked in disbelief.

"None whatsoever," he responded firmly. "If I focused on how well I was doing in terms of results-oriented goals, I'd probably slow down just like you did. But, instead, I've focused on the behavior-oriented goal of constantly increasing my rate of failure. I have complete and total faith that if I set my failure goals high enough, and do my best in each and every sales situation, then the successes will come. And they always do."

"I understand, but it's still going to take some getting used to."

"It took a while for me, too. And it took even longer for Elaine to get on board with the idea, but once she embraced it, there's been no stopping her!"

"How does Elaine get to apply the concept?" I asked.

"Well, she owns three galleries now, two in San Diego and one in Santa Barbara."

"She owns them?" I stammered.

"Yes, with a total of forty-five salespeople who all have countless opportunities to *go for no* everyday with every customer that enters the store. Believe it or not, research shows that eighty-five percent of all interactions between retail salespeople and shoppers end without the salesperson ever asking for a buying decision. Eighty-five percent! Believe me when I tell you, a huge part of Elaine's success has come from the way she's trained her people. No one walks out of an Elaine Bratton Gallery without saying *no* at least once."

The Science of Setting " NO" Goals

Here is the process for setting "*NO*" GOALS...

❶ First, use your current closing ratio to determine the number of sales opportunities you need to make to achieve the number of *yes's* you want for the week*. For example, if your standard closing ratio is 10%, and you want to make two sales, then you would need to sell to twenty people at your current rate of closing.

*Always set your "no" goals on a <u>daily</u> and/or <u>weekly</u> basis. Monthly goals provide us with too much 'imaginary' time to correct.

❷ At this point you have three options:

Option A...

If you subtract your anticipated number of yes's from your total sales opportunities, you arrive at your minimum '*no*' goal for the week. In this case: 20 - 2 = <u>18</u>.

Option B...

To play it safe, just make 20 your *no goal*
to insure your chances for success.

Option C...

Plan for a sales increase by increasing the number of *no's* you're going to get. For example, if you'd like a 30% increase for the week, multiply 18 (your minimum *no* goal) by 1.30 (30% up). 18 x 1.30 = 23.4. And since you always round up, that would make 24 your *no* goal for the week.

Option "A" keeps you from having bad weeks that occur because you get off to a great start and then slack off. Option "B" builds in a 10% increase in the number of calls and will provide a safety net for hitting your goal and probably a small increase. And Option "C" will create a sales explosion to whatever level you desire!

"Yes is the destination, NO is how you get there!"

Chapter Twenty...

When You're Hot, You're Hot!

"That's another benefit to setting "*no*" goals; you get built-in protection from prematurely ending a hot streak," he continued. "When salespeople hit a streak of yes's, the worst thing they can do is back off and slack off, but that's exactly what they usually do. But when you're going for *no* and you hit a hot streak of yes's, you actually step up your sales attempts to hit your *no* goal. Would a manager of a baseball team keep his star player out of a game because he was on a hot streak?"

"No," I replied.

"So then why would a salesperson sit himself or herself down when they're hot? It doesn't make any sense! You never want to lose your success momentum! When you were three for three, Eric, what did you do?"

"I took myself out of the game."

"Precisely. However, if you were *going for no* you would have been behind your goal and would have kept yourself in the game. We'll never know what kind of week you might have had."

"Hey, don't rub it in!" I said in mock anger.

"I want to rub it in, rub it in till it hurts! If it stings badly enough maybe you'll change your behavior."

"Don't worry, it stings plenty," I assured my twin.

Chapter Twenty One...

Next!

"You've probably heard this before, but it's one of the best examples of the relationship between failure and success that I know of. Abraham Lincoln had less than one year of formal schooling, failed in business twice, and lost eight of the ten elections he was in before winning the presidency in 1860. But is he remembered for his failures? No. He's remembered for saving the Union, abolishing slavery and being a man of great integrity and courage. Where would this nation be if Lincoln had a below average failure quotient?"

"Failure quotient?" I repeated.

"Yes. Each of us has our own personal *failure quotient*. In other words, how many times is a person willing to fail before succeeding? How many times are they willing to get knocked down and then get back up, knowing that they are almost certain to get knocked back down again? How much failure can they endure on the road to success?

"Perhaps the single most important factor that determines if a person will achieve everything they want in life, or simply settle for crumbs, is their failure quotient. Fortunately for the United States of America, Abraham Lincoln had a very high failure quotient!"

"I guess mine is fairly low. If I get three or four *no's* in a row, I stop for a donut," I chuckled.

"Did you know that R.H. Macy failed seven times to get his department store chain off the ground before he finally succeeded? Do you know the type of rejection Harland Sanders withstood when he started Kentucky Fried Chicken? Here's a guy who turns sixty-five and gets his first retirement check, only to discover it's not enough to live on. So he goes on the road and spends the next two years trying to sell owners of fast food restaurants on the idea of using his chicken recipe, and in that two year time, how many restaurants do you think he signed up?"

"I don't know."

"Zero. Not a one! Any normal person would have quit, but the "Colonel" wasn't normal; *he was extraordinary*. He keeps going, he gets better at his presentation, and finally he gets one acceptance. And then another, and another, and then another. I guarantee you, the taste of success he enjoyed at that point wasn't sweet... it was finger licking good!

"We can never let the word '*no*' devastate us. Think for a moment what it must be like to be a doctor. Every doctor knows that eventually, someday, they are going to lose a patient. Now what if every doctor, when they finally did lose a patient, said, *That's it! I'm done! I've failed and I'm through with medicine!* What would happen?"

"Pretty soon we'd have no doctors left," I answered.

"That's right. That's why in medical school, every doctor is taught the magic word they need for when they lose a patient, so they can get past the pain and keep going."

"What's the word?" I asked.

"Simple. The magic word is... *next!*" When a doctor loses a patient, they must be able to focus on their next patient, they must be able to move on; it's the only rational approach! But what do most of us do when we have a failure? We analyze it and languish over it and let ourselves get buried by it, when what we should do when something doesn't go our way is to simply say *next*, and move on."

"You make it sound easy."

"It isn't easy, but like everything else in life, it becomes easier with practice. "

"I wish I knew where my reluctance to hear *no* came from. I've tried to pinpoint it, but I really don't know."

"It doesn't matter where it came from!" he exclaimed. "The underlying reasons that people become afraid of rejection are countless; the way they were raised, an early traumatic sales experience...*who knows and who cares!* All I know is that inspirational CDs cannot coax your fears away, threats won't scare them away, and ignoring your fear won't make it go away on its own. The only way is to learn to '*numb*' yourself to *no*."

"You mean to ignore it?"

"No, I mean just the opposite. Numbing yourself to *no* isn't about ignoring it; it's about *experiencing* it so often that it eventually loses its power over you. Do the thing you fear..."

"...and the fear will go away," I finished.

"Yes. Just remember, Eric, that Lincoln is remembered for his accomplishments, not his failures. Babe Ruth is remembered for his record 714 homers, not his 1330 strikeouts, which was also a record! When everything in life is over and done with, no one will remember your failures, just your successes. And neither will you."

And with that, my mirror image shifted his attention to the activity of flying the plane, and we began our gradual descent toward Monterey.

Chapter Twenty Two...
A Morning at the Beach

It was still pitch black when the phone rang. I rolled over and fumbled the receiver, pulling it to my ear.

"Yes?" I managed.

"Good morning!" a voice said cheerfully. "This is your five o'clock wake up call!"

Wake up call? It took me several seconds to remember where I was, but then it all hit me: it was Saturday morning and I was in a suite at the Inn at Spanish Bay, set among groves of tall Monterey pines overlooking the Pacific Ocean. And I was about to play Pebble Beach!

I scrambled out of bed, showered and dressed, then headed down to the lobby. It was amazing how much energy one could have when one was about to play golf.

Eric strode in shortly afterwards and we made our way to the elegant restaurant and ordered breakfast.

"Sleep well?" Eric asked, digging into his eggs benedict.

"Yes, great," I responded.

"Good. I don't want there to be any excuses for why I kick your behind on the course this morning!"

"Oh, so that's how it's going to be, huh? Care to place a little wager?" I responded.

"With what? You have no money, remember."

He had me there.

"But we could play for something else." he said with an air of intrigue.

"Like what?"

"Oh, let's say low man gets to sit in the audience this afternoon and high man gives the presentation."

I looked at him and realized that I couldn't tell if he was serious or not. "I thought you loved to speak to large groups."

"Where do you get that?"

"The jacket cover to your book," I responded.

"Well, don't believe everything you read," he said with a laugh. "The truth is, I'm scared to death on a stage. Every time I'm introduced, I ask myself why on earth I accepted the engagement. Sometimes I feel like my heart is going to literally pound right out of my chest!"

"Why do you do it then?"

"Remember, the comfort zone is never static. It's either expanding…"

"…Or shrinking," I finished.

"Exactly," he said. "I know the day I start giving in to my fears in one area of my life, it will only be a matter of time before it becomes easier to avoid other challenges as well."

*   *   *

We met Kurt and Cheryl at the first tee, where I was introduced as Edward, Eric's twin brother (as was decided over dinner the night before).

"It's nice to meet you, Edward," Cheryl said, offering her hand.

"Edward is thinking of going into sales," Eric told the pair, "so I was hoping the two of you don't mind if he picks your brain a little as you play."

"No problem," Kurt replied as we shook hands as well. "We do nothing but talk shop anyway."

I was given the honors of teeing off first and felt pretty good with my straight, if not overly long drive. It soon became clear, however, that I wasn't going to be low man today as Kurt, Eric and Cheryl each out-drove me by about twenty yards.

Eric rode in the cart with Cheryl and I with Kurt.

"So you're thinking about going into sales, huh?" Kurt asked.

"Yep, and any tips you can share would be helpful."

"What kind of things do you want to know?"

"Well, what I really want is your take on the impact my brother's concepts have had on you and if you'd recommend them."

"By *concepts* you mean...?"

"I mean the idea of going for *no* rather than yes, increasing your failure quotient, that kind of stuff."

"Yeah, it does seem kind of weird at first, doesn't it?"

"Yes, it does. I know it worked for him; I've seen his house! But does it work for the average person?"

"Not for very long..." Kurt said.

This was not the answer I expected, but soon Kurt's true meaning became clear.

"...because within a short period of time, anyone who adopts his strategies stops being average," he continued. "When I first started working for your brother, I suffered from a bad case of Pike Syndrome. Have you ever heard of the Pike Syndrome?"

"I don't think so."

"A group of scientists at an aquarium in Canada did an experiment where they placed a large pike and some small minnows in a glass tank and separated them with a glass partition. The scientists watched this hungry pike repeatedly batter its nose against the invisible glass barrier for hours until the pike finally gave up. Then the scientists removed the glass partition, and what do you think happened?"

"Bye-bye minnows!"

"Nope. The pike stayed on its side of the tank, swimming in circles with lunch just inches away, restrained by only an imagined barrier. The pike had conditioned itself through hours of nose bumping to stay within its own self-imposed limitations.

"Most people are no different from pike," he continued. "They have bad experiences, bang their noses a few times and learn how to quit. Then they find themselves in a new situation, where there are no real barriers, where they can eat all the minnows they want, but do they? No. They restrain themselves within their own imaginary walls. When I started work for CopyQuest, that was me. But your brother changed the way I think, sell and live. I owe him a deep debt of gratitude."

"Because he taught you how to succeed?"

"No. Because he taught me to *enjoy* bumping my nose!"

Chapter Twenty Three...
You Don't Want to Buy Insurance, Do You?

The sun lifted itself higher in the sky and the beauty of Pebble Beach and the Monterey Peninsula was almost overwhelming. After nine holes, it was clear that the other me had no greater than a six handicap, while I would have to struggle to stay in double digits.

At the tenth hole, Eric suggested that we switch carts so I could have an opportunity to spend some time learning from Cheryl as well.

"I assume you're into this concept of failing more, too," I began.

"Absolutely! Studies show that as many as 80% of all salespeople don't make it through their first year for the simple reason that they failed to make enough calls. That's it. Nothing else."

"I always operated under the assumption that the key to success was skill and ability," I replied.

"Skill is highly overrated!" Cheryl laughed. "Don't get me wrong, Edward. When I first started in sales, I attended lots of training programs to polish my skills. The problem was that I didn't spend enough time applying them! While I was busy getting smarter, many people with far less talent and ability zoomed right by me. Eventually it became clear that a motivated person who was willing to get in front of enough people and simply tell their story would almost always outsell the 'sales pro' with the slick closes and fancy techniques. Let me give you an example.

"There was an insurance company in Chicago that called in a consultant to analyze why their profits were declining. The company was averaging only two and half sales per agent per month, and they were at wits end. So the consultant comes in and immediately puts his finger on the problem. He tells them, '*Your only problem is that you are not calling on enough people.*'

"Well, this solution was way too simple for the top executives at the company. After all, they'd paid this consultant *big money* and they wanted him to discover a *big problem!* So the consultant said, *'I'll prove it to you!'* He took a group of their salespeople, a cross-section of the sales force from best to worst, and told them, *'Effective today, you're going to start selling policies door to door in neighborhoods where you don't know a soul. There will be no leads provided. There will be no qualifying of prospects. And, when the person opens the door, you must start the sales call with the following words: 'You don't want to buy any life insurance, do you?'* Their mission was simply to see how many people they could repeat that message to every day. That was it! Needless to say, the salespeople were a bit skeptical."

"I can imagine. So, what happened?"

"The approach failed," she said matter-of-factly.

"Of course," I replied knowingly.

"Yep. Fifty-nine out of every sixty people they approached said, *You're right! I don't want to buy life insurance, so get lost!* But one out of every sixty said, *As a matter of fact, I do need insurance. Come on in and sign me up!*"

"One out of sixty isn't a very good closing ratio."

"You'd be right if it took a month to see 60 prospects, but with the consultant's approach, the average salesperson found that it only took about eight hours to approach 60 people with their *you don't want insurance* message. As a result, they immediately began averaging about one sale a day!"

"Wow! And the company was saved, right?"

"Yes. Approaching enough people with your offer, even with the most negative message imaginable, can save whole companies and entire careers. You see, if you truly want to accelerate your sales performance, you have to *fail faster!*"

"That reminds me of this telemarketing guru I heard about," I interjected. "He recommends that phone solicitors ask customers in the first ten seconds if they have interest in hearing about the product they're selling. If the customer says no, then they politely say thank you and move on rather than going through their entire pitch. As a result they make ten times as many calls, but only invest their time making their complete sales pitch to prospects who have just qualified themselves."

"It's the same basic premise," Cheryl replied. "You know, when you mine for gold, you don't really look for the gold, you remove the dirt. Selling and gold mining are very much alike. It's the people who remove the most dirt, who work their way through the greatest number of *no's*, who ultimately discover the greatest number of *golden yes's!*"

Chapter Twenty Four...
No Doesn't Mean Never

After we finished the eighteenth hole, Eric suggested we have lunch at the Pebble Beach clubhouse, and soon I was enjoying the best BLT I've ever tasted.

"So, did Kurt and Cheryl answer your questions?" Eric asked.

"Yes, they did," I said, nodding.

"Good. Well, if you don't mind, I have a question I'd like to ask each of you," Eric said, looking to Kurt and Cheryl.

"Sure, of course," they said in unison.

"It's the same question for both of you. The question is: besides the basic concept of going for *no* and increasing your failure rate, what is *the* one piece of advice you'd offer to anyone who wants to be outrageously successful at selling?"

"Ladies first!" Kurt said to Cheryl with a devious smile.

"Gee, thanks for putting me on the hot seat!" Cheryl kidded.

"This is not a test, guys," Eric reassured them. "I just want my brother to learn everything he can from your experience."

"Well," Cheryl began, "the best piece of advice I can offer is to learn that *no doesn't mean never, it means not yet.* Statistically, research shows that forty-four percent of salespeople give up after one *no*. Twenty-two more give up after the *second no*. Fourteen percent more give up after the *third no*. Twelve more give up after the *fourth no*. What does that come to?"

I did some quick math in my head. "Ninety-two percent," I replied.

"Correct. Ninety-two percent of all salespeople give up without asking for the sale a fifth time, but research also shows that sixty percent of all customers *say no four times* before they finally say yes. That means the quickest way to separate yourself from the rest of the pack is to get at least five *no's* from everyone you try to sell to!"

"And you track that?" I asked.

"Absolutely!" she responded. "I can look in my records and tell you exactly how many times each prospect has turned me down. I never leave a prospect's office without getting at least one *no*, because a *no* is always better than getting a '*let me think about it.*'"

"In what way could that be better?" I asked, intrigued.

"Because when I get someone to say *no*, I can immediately move to the next step which is to ask, '*why?*' *Let me think about it* teaches me absolutely nothing, but if they say *no* and I follow up with *why*, now I'm on the verge of discovering what I need to do next to make the sale."

"And she usually does," Eric added with a smile.

"When a potential customer says *no*, most salespeople hear *never*... but what I hear is *not yet!*" Cheryl said in conclusion.

"That reminds me of the Allen Breed story," Kurt said.

"Who is Allen Breed?" I asked.

"Do you have an air-bag in your car?" Kurt asked.

"Sure."

"Well, that air-bag is there because of Allen Breed. Back in 1967, Allen Breed began offering the air-bag sensors he invented to Detroit automakers, but the big three told him to get lost. They weren't interested in such an expensive item they perceived as unnecessary. But Breed didn't go away. Not only did he keep pestering the automakers, but he also invested huge quantities of time and money lobbying congress. Finally, almost twenty years after he started, congress passed legislation mandating the use of airbags."

"Twenty years! That's some kind of failure quotient!"

"You haven't heard anything yet," Eric interjected, nodding for Kurt to continue.

"It still took another ten years before his first big sale was made," Kurt said. "In 1995, almost thirty years after Breed's first rejection,

Breed Technologies sold twenty-three million air-bag sensors for a *net profit* of almost *one-hundred and twenty million dollars!*"

"I think it's fair to say that most people would have heard *no*," Eric said, "but Allen Breed chose to hear *not yet*."

"And that story brings up another question," said Cheryl. "Did Breed earn one-hundred twenty million dollars in 1995? Or did he earn four million a year for every year he was willing to hear *no*?"

Chapter Twenty Five...
The Big Enchilada

"Okay, Kurt, you're up," Eric said, shifting in his chair and turning his attention to the tanned, handsome salesman.

"Well, I'd have to say my advice would be this... *If you're going to fail, fail big!*" Kurt stated.

"Elaborate on that," Eric encouraged.

"What I mean is simply this," Kurt continued. "Common sense says that if you're going to get a *no* from somebody, get it from the client who needs twenty copiers, not just two. Get rejected by the purchasing agent from the company that buys forty thousand gallons of cleaning solution every month, not just forty.

"Think about the numbers for a moment. If I call on one hundred accounts that each have the potential to lease two copiers from me, and my closing ratio is ten percent, then I end up with twenty units out the door, right? But by focusing on accounts with the potential to lease twenty copiers, I only needed to close *one sale* to get the same twenty units!"

"So you're saying to avoid small accounts," I summarized.

"I have nothing against calling on small accounts. Small accounts grow up to become large accounts, and they can often be more lucrative. I'm just suggesting that there are many salespeople who intentionally avoid going for large sales because they're afraid of blowing the big one. This is silly! In the end a *no* is a *no* regardless of the size of the account, but the rewards for the yes's are huge!"

Chapter Twenty Six…
Failing Exponentially

Eventually it became time for Kurt and Cheryl to turn the tables on my twin.

"So, Eric, it's your turn. What do you think is the single most important factor in becoming outrageously successful at selling?" Cheryl asked.

"I've spent the last three days espousing my views on the subject. I'm sure Edward has had enough of my advice."

"I can never get enough of you," I said with a chuckle.

"Okay, if you insist," he began with a smile. "But understand that my viewpoints these days come from a management perspective, and I'd like to offer two.

"For starters, I'd say that a primary key to creating outrageous success is to understand the need to *fail exponentially*. After all, one person can only fail so fast. Great leaders help *everyone* in the organization understand the need to fail faster.

"Take a company with a sales force of one hundred, for example. Imagine that each of the organization's salespeople were to increase the number of *no's* they received by five a day; not the number of people they sell to, but the number of no's they get during their current sales opportunities."

"Like Cheryl was saying before," I offered, "getting a *no* or even multiple *no's* from every person you sell to."

"Exactly. When you do the math, it would look like this: one hundred salespeople multiplied by two hundred working days a year multiplied by five additional *no's* per day would equal *one hundred thousand additional no's per year*… without increasing costs whatsoever! The impact on organizational results is monumental!"

"Kind of like the classic Thomas Edison example," I added. "You know, where the newspaper reporter approaches Edison and asks him what it feels like to have failed ten thousand times to invent the light bulb, to which Edison replied, *I haven't failed ten thousand times - I've simply discovered ten thousand ways that will not work!*"

"Yes," Eric replied, "but what most people don't hear about is what happened next. Edison went out and hired a bunch of inventors to work in his laboratory with him, knowing full well that every inventor he hired was nowhere near as smart or as talented as he was. Why did he do this? Because, even with ten thousand 'failures' under his belt, Edison didn't think he was failing fast enough on his own. Edison is the poster child for what can be accomplished when you put failing bigger, failing faster and failing exponentially together. He literally lit the world!

"Exponential failure requires someone in the organization to be an exponent, in other words an advocate or spokesman, of the failure concept and to champion it. But I can't begin to tell you how many executives I've seen who reach the top and suddenly forget what got them there. They start trying to avoid failure, and when a leader is afraid to fail, everyone in the organization knows it. Not only do people sense it but they figure that if you're afraid of something, there's a good chance it's something they should be afraid of, too."

Chapter Twenty Seven...
Celebrating Success and Failure

"Eric, you said there were two things leaders can do to create outrageous success. What's the second?" I asked.

"The second is to *reward people for their failures, not just their successes*," he responded. "Everyone runs over to congratulate people for their sales successes, but how often do we go out of our way to congratulate people for their failures?"

"Virtually never," I said.

"Exactly. In the book, *The Greatest Management Principle* author Michael LeBoeuf says quite accurately that *you don't get what you beg for, wish for, or pray for, you get what you reward.* Well if you truly believe that seeing lots of potential customers ultimately leads to success and you want that behavior to continue, then you should reward the behavior of seeing lots of people, regardless of the immediate results. Don't get me wrong; I'm all in favor of rewarding people for their successes, but not to the exclusion of recognizing the people who've displayed a true willingness *and wantingness* to fail. You mustn't neglect them just because their yes's haven't fallen into place yet.

"At CopyQuest, we recognize the top ten salespeople with a 'Producers Pin' award," Eric continued, "but we also recognize the ten salespeople in the organization with the greatest number of failed attempts with what we call the '*Go for No!*' award. And, if I recall correctly, Cheryl and Kurt made both lists."

"It's funny," Cheryl said, "but the '*Go for No!*' trophy meant more to me than the Producers Pin."

"Really?" I said in disbelief.

"Yeah. The Producers Pin was recognition of my external achievement, but the '*Go for No!*' trophy was validation of my *internal desire.*"

"I feel the same way," Kurt added. "And, besides, we get recognized for our production every week via our paychecks!"

"What's interesting," Eric said, "is that we thought we were creating two separate awards, but over time, they're becoming almost mirrors of each other."

"That's because we've caught on to the concept that winning a '*Go for No!*' award almost assures that you'll end up with a Producers Pin. Or, put another way," Kurt concluded, "***Yes is the destination, No is how you get there!***"

Chapter Twenty Eight…
The Blink of an Eye

The helicopter touched down on the roof of the Moscone Center in the heart of downtown San Francisco where the annual conference for the International Society of Sales Executives was being held. We were greeted and then quickly escorted to a small green room where the speakers prepared and relaxed before taking the stage.

"How many people are there going to be in the audience?" I asked our escort.

"About 3,000," he responded.

I immediately looked to Eric who managed a smile in spite of the certain nervousness he must have been feeling. I had never spoken to any group larger than 20 people and could only imagine the butterflies my twin was attempting to get into formation.

Our escort left to go check on things, leaving Eric and me alone in the green room.

"You look deep in thought," I observed. "Last minute review?"

"I was just deciding what my final story should be. I think I'm going to talk about something that happened yesterday afternoon when I was in the office."

"Anything you'd like to share?"

"Sure. I had a salesman call me trying to sell me some permanent retirement property."

"Permanent retirement property? What in the heck does that mean?" I asked.

"It's the politically correct way of saying *grave site* in the year 2000. Anyway, I told him 'no thank you' and hung up. Ten minutes later, he called me back and said, '*You know, Mr. Bratton, your time on the planet earth is little more than the blink of an eye, but your time after that is forever.*'"

"That's a pretty good sales pitch. What did you say to that?"

"Let me put it this way: You and I are going to be spending eternity with Elaine, permanently retired on a beautiful hillside at Forest Lawn!" he laughed. "The whole experience made me think about how people say they want to go out a success. Have you ever heard the saying, 'I want to go out a winner?'"

"All the time. I've said it myself."

"I've said it, too, but I just realized how silly that is. Statistically speaking, if you're still challenging yourself until the day you die, then the odds are good that you'll *fail* at the very last thing you attempt. Imagine that... the last act of the most successful people in the world will be to fail!

"I've accomplished a lot already, Eric," my twin continued, "but I'm only thirty-eight. I figure I've still got another 40 years left in me, maybe more, in which to do great things. God only knows what successes are in my future, in *our* futures, but I'm 100 percent certain that whatever they may be, the only way to achieve them will be to continue risking, taking chances, and showing outrageous courage."

* * *

The escort returned and led us up some stairs at the side of the stage just as Eric was being introduced to the audience. We climbed to the top of the stairs, my body-double and I, and it was then that he leaned over and spoke softly in my ear. It was so soft that I could barely hear him over the roar of the crowd that was starting to welcome him.

"I don't think that your showing up here has happened by chance. I think you've been given a gift, the chance to see what your life could be like if you want it badly enough."

"But I'm not sure I'm as good as you," I responded.

"Oh, Eric, you still don't get it, do you? I'm not better than you... *I am you*... the you that you're supposed to be. I'm the vision of your potential, providing of course that you're willing to do what it takes. Yes, this has been a gift to you... *a gift I need you to accept!*"

He placed his arms around me and hugged me close, and as he did, I understood what he was saying. He was the potential of me, and as such, *he* needed *me* to overcome my self-imposed limitations or he would never exist.

Eric broke our embrace and headed toward the center of the stage to address the cheering crowd that awaited his message... *a message that would change their lives if they would allow it...* and a message that I knew could change mine as well.

Just then a man wearing headphones tapped me on the shoulder.

"Excuse me," he said, "but the cameraman says he's getting you in the shot. We need you to move off the stairs."

"Sure," I replied.

But as I turned, the heel of my shoe caught on the stair and I lost my balance. And as I fell in slow motion off the stairs toward the floor below, all I could think was... *not again!*

Chapter Twenty Nine…
Dorothy Goes Home

The first thing I remember was hearing Elaine telling someone *yes*, she still wanted to talk with Dr. Weiss again, and *yes* she remembered she had met with him just last night, and *yes* she realized it was Sunday morning. The girl did not take *no* for an answer easily!

The second thing I remember was feeling the slow throbbing pain behind my right ear.

I opened my eyes to find myself lying in a hospital bed, Elaine deep in conversation with a nurse and Carl sitting nearby reading a *People Magazine*.

"Aren't you supposed to be counting beans somewhere?" I said to Carl. "It's the middle of tax season still, isn't it?"

Carl looked up from his magazine and Elaine spun around, running to the side of the bed, tears welling up in her eyes.

"I was so worried," was all she could manage.

"What day is it?" I asked.

"Sunday. Somehow or other you fell out of bed and hit your head early Thursday morning."

"I've been out for four days!" I said in disbelief.

"Yep. The doctor thinks you hit the nightstand first and then the floor. The double impact gave you a serious concussion. We've all been worried sick," Carl said with a relieved smile.

The nurse returned and took my pulse and other vital signs, informing us that everything appeared normal and that the doctor would be by shortly. In the meantime, she said, I should rest.

For the next twenty minutes I recounted the entire story of waking up ten years in the future and meeting myself, about what I had learned and the realizations I had had about my career and my life. I even told Carl about the round of golf I shot at Pebble Beach.

He said it sounded wonderful, and that we should make plans to play there together soon, after tax season of course.

As we waited for the doctor to arrive, I suddenly remembered the page I had ripped from the book, but the ensuing search for my proof turned up nothing.

It all seemed so real. It was almost impossible to believe it was a dream.

But that's all it had been… nothing more than a dream.

Epilogue…
Six Months Later

September is often the hottest month of the year in Southern California, and this year was no exception.

I hopped out of the Cutlass, glanced at my watch, grabbed my briefcase and headed quickly toward the entrance of the Callaway Golf corporate headquarters. My notes indicated I had called on the golf club giant four previous times and had collected a total of seventeen *no's* from three different people.

Since returning to work following my concussion, I had claimed the number one ranking in overall sales three of the last five months and was in serious contention for salesman of the year. I had earned more money during the last six months than I had in all of the previous year. The most important statistic, however, the one I was proudest of, was my heavy lead in the number of times I had *failed* to lease a copier. I knew in my heart that as long as I led in that category, nothing could stop me.

The receptionist led me to the vice president's office, a man by the name of Robert Merrill. I was greeted, offered coffee and asked to sit. This was my first meeting with Merrill.

"I hate to start on a negative note, young man," Merrill began, "but you're wasting your time calling on us. We're very happy with our current supplier, and we're locked into a three-year deal. But you seem determined, so give me your best 15-minute spiel," he said, removing his Rolex and laying it on the desk to let me know I was on the clock.

As the allotted time expired, Merrill politely told me *no* for the second, third and fourth times. But he said he liked some of what I had to say and suggested that I schedule a follow up with his secretary, adding they weren't as locked in as he might have suggested.

It had taken five meetings with four people, plus 21 *no's* and counting, but the window of opportunity was finally opening as I knew it eventually would.

As I stood to leave, I noticed something that stopped me dead in my tracks. There on the wall was a picture of the seventh green at the La Costa Resort.

"You play golf?" Merrill asked.

"Not as much as I'd like, but I get out a couple of times a month," I said, still staring at the photo.

"That's the seventh green at La Costa," he said. "I'm a member there; we should play."

"I'll bet this picture was taken from the balcony of your house, just down the hall from the master bedroom," I said with confidence.

"As a matter of fact, it was! How could you possibly know that?"

Because I've been there, I wanted to say.

"Just a guess," I replied.

"It's a wonderful house. I'm going to miss it."

"You're moving?"

"Oh, not for several years," Merrill replied. "I still have a lot I want to accomplish here, but my wife has always had a thing for Scottsdale. That's where we'll retire."

I reached into my pocket and pulled out one of my cards. I wrote my home phone number on the back and handed it to Merrill.

"When you're ready to sell, don't bother calling a real estate agent. I'm the person who's going to buy your house."

"You seem certain," Merrill replied.

"Not just certain," I replied, "It's my destiny."

Then, as I headed for the door, I heard Merrill call out, "Wait, you dropped something!"

I looked down. There, under the chair I'd been sitting in, was a folded sheet of paper. Even before I walked over and picked it up, I knew what it was. It was the page I had ripped from Eric's book... my book... *the book I was just beginning to write.*

Follow Richard & Andrea at:

Facebook.com/Goforno

Twitter.com/Goforno

YouTube.com/Courageous1s

Linkedin.com/In/Goforno

Enjoyed the book? Just wait until you see the NEW Go for No!® movie!

Featuring...

- Tony Alessandra
- Richard Brooke
- Bob Burg
- Jack Canfield
- Jim Cathcart
- John Milton Fogg
- Randy Gage
- Lisa Jimenez
- Art Jonak
- Pam Lontos
- W Mitchell
- Nido Qubein
- Wayne Allyn Root
- "Rudy" Ruettiger
- Chris Widener
- Larry Winget

And over 40 others!

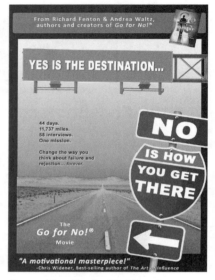

Created by *Go for No!*® authors Richard Fenton & Andrea Waltz, this amazing personal development documentary let's you hop in the passenger seat as they drive nearly 12,000 miles across America interviewing top performers to learn their secrets for achieving massive success. Also comes with a link to over 20 hours of audio interviews!

"This DVD should be sent out to everyone - especially in this economic downturn. It changes your perception in terms of what is truly possible. I'm pumped!"

- ***Laura Gross***, *President*
no,no,no, YES! Inc.

Available at: **www.GoForNo.com**

Quotes from the Go for No!® Movie...

- *"If you want to be confident in confronting a potential 'NO', ask for a lot of stuff so that you get rejected enough to know you can handle it, and that you didn't die."*
  -Jack Canfield

- *"Had I really given up, had I believed that 'NO' meant the end of the world, I think I would have taken a completely different course in life."*
  -Nido Qubein

- *"Talent can always be learned, but the determination, the perseverance, that's where most people fall down."*
  -Randy Gage

- *"I eat no for breakfast. 'No' is the opening dialogue of a conversation. That's all no is."*
  -Wayne Allyn Root

- *"When somebody says 'No, I'm not interested', your response should be, 'I'm closer!'"*
  -Richard Brooke

- *"I was brought up on the philosophy that if you don't ask, you don't get. And if you don't get, ask again! Maybe they misunderstood the question!"*
  -Tony Alessandra

- *"The only 'NO' that really matters is the one you say to yourself."*
  -W Mitchell

- *"NOs really teach you stuff. I'm not sure that yesses do. Yeses make you feel great, you got the result, but I think we probably learn more from the NOs."*
  -John Milton Fogg

- *"I hear 'NO' a lot, and I'll probably start to worry the day I stop hearing NOs, because I'll know that's the day I'm not continuing to progress."*
  -Bob Burg

- *"It's all about transforming our relationship to the word "No" and transforming our relationship to rejection."*
  -Lisa Jimenez

- *"There is no such thing as rejection."*
  -Margie Aliprandi

- *"I tell our team, 'Fail at something every day.'"*
  –Art Jonak

- *"If you're not succeeding fast enough, you're probably not failing fast enough, and you can't have one without the other."*
  -Joe Malarkey® (George Campbell)

- *"About half the stuff I do is wrong. I mean that's just how it works in life. That's how it works for everybody."*
  -Larry Winget

Get Your Copy of the Go for No!® DVD Movie Today!

www.GoForNo.com

Now Available! The Complete Go for No!®
'Mastery' Program on 3 Audio CDs!

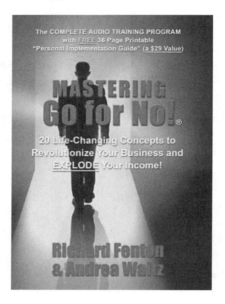

THIS IS <u>NOT</u> SIMPLY THE BOOK ON CD!

Three years in the making, this is Rich & Andrea's complete program for turning the negative, draining effects of failure and rejection into a POWERFUL POSITIVE in your business and your life! Applying the 20 proven concepts taught in this groundbreaking audio CD training program will:

- *Increase your sales and prospecting activity...*
- *Remove negative feelings about hearing "NO"...*
- *Eliminate business "slumps"...*
- *And <u>EXPLODE</u> your income!*

Comes with a printable 36-page Personal Implementation Guide.

Available at:

www.GoForNo.com

Change Your Programming, Change Your Life!

It has been said that the word "NO" has destroyed more dreams than any other force on the planet. But it doesn't have to be that way!

Featuring over 100 high-impact 'reprogramming statements' set to nine different music soundtracks (similar to affirmations but far more powerful), this CD literally helps you **REPROGRAM YOUR THINKING** around the topics of failure and rejection.

Because it's not enough to simply sit back and 'hope' your negative attitudes about failure and rejection will shift to a more powerful mindset overnight. That's why Go for No!® authors Richard Fenton & Andrea Waltz created this amazing CD!

Available at:

www.GoForNo.com

Andrea Waltz & Richard Fenton...

The Perfect Speakers for Your Next Meeting or Conference!

For the last decade Richard Fenton & Andrea Waltz have been sharing their empowering *Go For No!®* message to hundreds of organizations, including **American Express, Discovery Channel, Primerica, Kodak, Samsonite, Arbonne International, JCPenney,** and many others.

Based on the concepts in the book, people will learn...

- *To develop a more empowering definition of failure*
- *The primary restraining force that holds people back in life*
- *Why their NO-Quotient™ (N.Q.) is more important than their I.Q.*
- *Why they must have NO-Goals™ to reach their full potential*
- *What it takes to outperform 92% of the people in the world*
- *How to stop selling from "their own wallets"*
- *And much more!*

Available as a 45-90 minute keynote presentation or as a half-day workshop to fit your specific needs, your team will come away with a more empowering perspective for achieving breakthrough performance!

For more information on Having Richard & Andrea
speak at your event, visit: www.GoforNoKeynote.com

Or call: **800-290-5028**

Or Email: Info@GoForNo.com